Songs of Hellenes

Sarah Winek

BookLeaf
Publishing

India | USA | UK

Presentation by *BookLeaf Publishing*

Web: www.bookleafpub.com

E-mail: info@bookleafpub.com

ISBN: 9789367398814

First edition 2024

PREFACE

We look to the stars at night, from whence we came.

They watch each soul's destiny unfold on Earth, hidden under the velveteen cloak of night. They whisper – to the ever-changing moon and amongst themselves – of the unknown secrets we humans keep locked away, deep inside our mortal hearts.

Only the stars know the wishes we pray for. Only the stars know our fate.

S. J. W

Pandora

I opened the box.
So what?
I opened the box –
Why the shock?

You carved me cunning,
You curved my hips and now curse,
You made me a woman.

I am but a girl.
I wanted to look –
Is that such a crime?

I opened the box,
Curiosity, had me hooked –
You would have done the same.
Now I'm damned, for all time.

Persephone

Six months on Earth, time passing.
A daughter's reprieve from gloomy tombs,
A Mother's love everlasting.

Together – we harvest the farming,
Mighty horses plough earthly hills.
Six months on Earth – time passing.

I observe her mood darkening,
'Sixteen days' she whispers – face broken, she
cries.
My Mother's love everlasting.

Ground stirring – husband waiting.
My return inevitable, he knows it.
Six months on Earth, time passing.

Another melancholy chorus of Grecian
summers.
My mother weeps, her tears –
salty stains of regret.

My Mother's love is everlasting.

Athena

Worship, pray to me.
Hateful heroes spill blood, coveting battlefields.
I'll set your mortal soul free.

Or – will you live?
Rush from death, with his constraining promises
of eternity –
Worship men; pray to me.

You – minuscule homosapien clichés,
Prometheus's tragedy –
Ash and blood condensed as one,
I'll set your mortal soul free.

I salivate in triumph at all human frailty,
Squabbles amongst men bore me yet, I still
demand.
Worship, bow down and pray to me.

War incited over male pride, the root of human
savagery.
They – fight! territorial ants over sickly nectar
I'll set your mortal soul free.

Forget the transgressions of your enemy.
Lie soldier – here. Forsaken breath gasp –
Worship. Pray to me,
I'll set your mortal soul free.

Echo

It really wasn't worth the pain, pain, pain,
My echo, this unworthy curse.
My tattered heart hangs in shame.
Though, I mustn't, mustn't, mustn't – oh pest!
Leave me be – Hades, steal my woe.
It really wasn't worth the pain – pain – pain.
If I could do things differently, hide my face in
vain –
Not let you see me, all lovestruck and teary.
My tattered heart hangs in shame.
Cruel Narcissus; foul vanity is your game.
Mocking sweet declarations of love, of love, of
love –
It really wasn't worth the pain – pain – pain.
I've considered my beauty, am I so plain?
I've lost my voice – an echo remains –
yet my tattered heart hangs in shame.
Why? I ask you. Not even a reply.
Why? Do you not love – me, me, me?
It really wasn't worth the pain, pain, pain –
My tattered heart hangs in shame.

Eurydice

Poor Orpheus, you stand here so true.
Your crestfallen eyes, cloaked like sunken ships
under the waning moon,
What will you do?

Sing of your sorrows, until night calls
I flee to the sanctuary of death's underground
palace.
Poor Orpheus, you stand here, so true.

Eager tears trickle past the curve of your cheek,
settle softly on sparkling dew.
Yearning to wash away death's rules.
What will you do?

Melodies of love, you sing.
Illuminating the innocence of young lovers who
lie under the stars,
Poor Orpheus, you stand here, so true.

Singing saccharine ballads, flatter me as your
muse.
Fret not! Love? – it's fickle as April skies.
What will you do?

By turning. By looking. By glancing.
You sealed our doom.
Opaque souls swirl around us; it is time to leave.

Poor Orpheus. You stand here, so true,
What will you do?

Circe

We have one more day.
Idle fingertips of mine, carelessly fondle the hair
on your chest.
Everything means nothing, unless you stay.

The journey is arduous, come here and lay?
Let our nakedness make the watchful moon shy,
turn away her face
We have one more day.

The essence of us, will forever convey
our serendipitous love, my Odysseus.
Everything means nothing, unless you stay.

The island of Ithaca, with her unremarkable
shores, far away.
Common, chalky sands, behold! My exotic
dunes.
It's love, just wait.

The fates, foretell misfortune and death and
decay.
Bind my lips to yours; kiss me now – forget who
you were.
Everything means nothing – unless you stay.

Penelope. She doesn't burn for you like I do.
Please delay.
Orion's belt cannot contain our fire
and yet we have one more day,

Everything means nothing unless you stay.

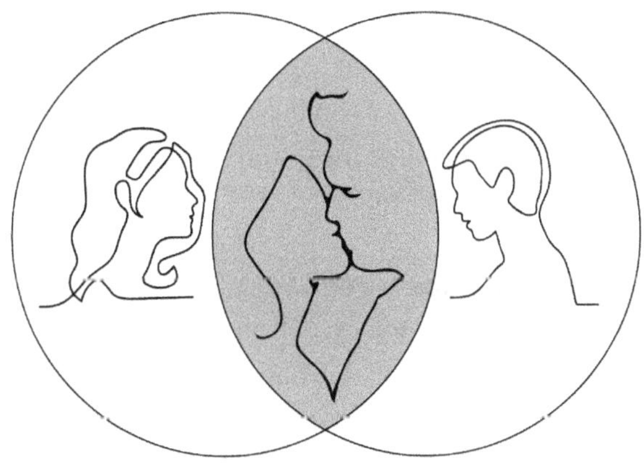

Medea

A promise whispered,
On cold marble steps.
'More than life itself' you told me –
When I'd asked you – how much?

How much – did you ever love me?
How naive did I seem.
You smiled. I believed you.
You lied, said you would make me your Queen.

You said, we would leave this labyrinth.
Sail together, far away to the East,
Beyond the scorched horizon of Crete,
You promised me freedom.

In return, a simple piece of string.
Your freedom – I won you.
Freedom from death. A Minotaur's prey.
You spill lies Theseus, perfidious Prince of
promises.

Penelope

Tapestried walls burst beneath their surface,
Seething with a loyal wife's love,
Crumbling under the weight of time's grasp.
He comes.
He waits.

Ships steal into unforgiving seas that surround
Ithacan shores.
None are the Argo.
None are you.

Black mast pinheads bob upon azure waves,
Tired, am I of longing for your return.
Consumed by fear.
He comes.
He waits.

I weave these fragile threads desperate to delay,
Unpicking them with false intentions –
I pray you will return before it's too late.

Oh no. He comes – Odysseus!

Hades

Swollen belly of the underworld,
Lord of the dead, am I.
King of death and despair.

I wait for you, I linger.
Chasing the shadows, waiting for a glimpse of
your milky, tender flesh –
sweetness that will soften a King's solitude.

Seek me out and you will find,
Knock at my door and I will lie down and weep
at your feet,
All will be given to you.
If only, you return.

Cerberus, my faithful servant, guard of the gates
of our kingdom.
Solemn as a coroner's first look, pining for his
Queen, who dances above.
Run, my bride.

Persephone, brutal winds blow you home.
Fast as flesh stiffens when death calls,
Your face, lovely as spring
No longer leave me alone.

Look your last glance,
At the brazen September sun,
Kiss goodbye to Demeter and her grain,
You belong to me.

Aphrodite

Love? You can keep it.
Love? A temporary insanity of the mind.
Love. Love. Love.

Is this all I am known for?
The purveyor of young lovers, old lovers
Forbidden lovers (*always the best*).

Rarely it lasts; stifled by the confines of
marriage,
Once eager promises of youth,
Now fade to grey, decay with a touch.

Man, Prometheus's prodigy.
Woman's misery.
For woman – a man's servant, at his mercy.

A wife. To love and obey.
Love, only for love's sake.
Love lasts for man, as long as
there's still youth in her face –

Isn't every beauty like love –
temporary.
Easily replaced.

The Fates

Golden is this thread of life,
Sits within woven strings,
Three women hold the power –
The destiny of everything, of everyone.

Clotho, the spinner of destiny,
Lachesis, disposer of lots,
Atropos, she who could not be turned,
Cuts your thread of life with her merciless blade,
And when your time is up –
You'll soon be forgotten.

The Muses

Known as the Nine,
Governors of men's hearts,
At the mercy of our pleasure,
Ruthlessly, we threaten to shred them apart.

First, we lull them with dreams,
Promises of immortality and masculine glory
heroes stories spilling blood from Scylla's lips
and fierce battles of Troy; such violent fables.

Hellenes shores and Hellenes hearts,
We are the keepers of wishes,
Holding secrets of long-forgotten youthful
longings,
Mortals, so full of lost wishes.

Pyramus & Thisbe

City of Queen Semiramis is where begins this
tragedy –
Obstacles come; they stifle love
Waiting for two young lovers,
Cursed by fate.

Love, forbidden.
Is the sweetest to taste.
The flame can be covered,
But burns brighter with haste –

Love hastens to covet,
Love hastens to have,
Love hastens to hold,
Love hastens to remain hidden.

The handsome youth Pyramus
And the beauty that was his Thisbe,
Chemistry unseen –
Formed through a hole in the wall,

Kisses transmitted on paper scrolls,
Through concrete walls and cracks,
Whispers conspired through the wall with hopes
to elope –
No turning back.

Thisbe and Pyramus, to meet by the tomb –
So close did they come – to avoiding their
doom.
Dawn put out the stars,
There was no turning back.

Star crossed from the start,
So close and yet, so far apart,
in death – their reunion –
Together at last.

Hera

He visits me now.
He visits me then.
Desecrated our vows –
again, and again.

A swan, a stag, why even a fox!
My husband; the changeling.
Me; his long-suffering wife,
A pitied laughing stock.

Whores of false royalty
Girls, immortal and nymphs fair
Zeus, the *almighty*.
Why? he just doesn't care.

Me. Oh just his wife
hearing more rumours from Olympus.
I see the blushes when he laughs.
Fool, little does he know –

I belong to another.
A mortal! imagine, his face.
King of the Gods, a cuckold,
A laughing stock amongst the immortals,
His serendipitous fall from grace.

Cupid & Psyche

Zephyr kissed my throat this long night.
High on a hilltop under meteor skies,
red flames rise, a frightening sight,
I knew not, what unknown terrors awaited me.

Up I rose, like a ruffled dove's feather
into Zephyr's arms.
His winds carried me to golden meadows,
Immersed beside riverbanks, lit with moonlight.

I bathed naked in their waters,
Rhapsodic singing beckoned with the breeze,
Unseen, as my husband waited.
His face obscured; he watched me.

His shadow – I could not yet fully see,
tender was his touch.
Sudden, gentle fingers caress the small space in
the hollow of my back –

I turn, he begs me to not look,
I want to obey, feel his caress,
His icy fingers on my flesh.

I am the soul; he is the love that binds us –
Together as one under meteor skies.

Medusa

Medusa, the serpent,
Medusa, the maiden,
Medusa, the gorgon,
Raped by Poseidon.

Thrown from the protection of Athena's temple,
then
destroyed. Defiled.
Transformed into this beast –
Hideous and wild.

My fate, to murder all men,
who come to my lair,
Holding their poised murderous arrows –
Unafraid and unimpressed –
I shoot them dead with my glare.

Yet, my serpent heart still softens,
Not yet wholly
made of stone,
I'm not all
monster,
My struggles,
always
unknown.

Perseus

I hear the night as I dream,
Cloaked in Pegasus wings,
Curse Cassiopeia as her daughter waits –
My brute of a father, the immortal king.

Andromeda – a virgin bride.
'Tis true; her beauty renowned, yet –
destined to die.
The Gorgon Medusa, whose head I must
possess, to keep her alive.

What a chore, what a trip.
At the cusp of Argos's shore.
The Kraken –
I've seen him before.

When only a babe in a chest was I,
Helpless, an infant prince left to drown at sea,
Trapped in a wooden box sealed with Zeus's
shame.
My mother – Danae, and me.

Achilles

Strong beyond measure,
Kind beyond words,
His glorious head, a hidden weakness
that Thetis concealed from the world.

Achilles – an almighty warrior.
Unbeatable foe,
It took one shot –
From an unremarkable bow.

He falls; he bleeds.
Toppled by fate.
Atropos cut his thread –
He now waits at Hades' gate.

Fallen glory, fallen hero,
The man and the myth.
Fire amongst icy soldiers –
If only that arrow had missed.

Apollo

Blazing boy of the sun,
Steering a dozen golden stallions,
Laurel leaves crown his brow,
He chases the Moon from view.

Feeble stars flee, and the dark bursts into
scattered fragments as the light –
The light he commands pours from his
fingertips.
Night becomes day,
day turns to dusk.

Chasing the time as she flies –
as all things on earth turn to dust.

The Sirens

Men, thirsty men of mortal beauteous flesh – we
see you,
Come hither and play a while,
Come, see our seashells and shore –
Our jewels in the bay.

Fear not – our sweet song,
Fear not – our embrace,
We shall love any man we can touch forever,
Come, muscular mortal flesh of man,
Leave your oars awhile.

Come, see our lips soft as peonies,
Our breasts, soft to touch
We, offer restful Elysian respite for starved
sailors.
A haven for the weariest soul.

Strained are you men,
Salty tears of sweat, we smell
them drip from your chest –
Forget your home and take
refuge,
Our lonely siren's bequest.

Zeus

Lightening; ripples through the threads of my
veins.
Titans cower; Hermes trumpets my name –
Zeus. The Almighty!
Wife stealer, unpredictable tyrant of truth –
Olympian King am I.
Worshipped from cradle to grave,
around hearts of Greece and around again and
again.
Fear me, or love me –
I care not.
Your thoughts – insignificant, in the end.
It will be you that time forgot!
You – whose name and body crumble to bone.
Lie, under nameless headstones,
You, simple mortal
A forgotten relic – a little life, most
unremarkable.
Not I though, who will reign supreme.
I who command whom I please,
Have whom I please,
Do what I please,
I have no care as pride ignites my immortal
veins,
It is you that will carry,
The burden of my name.

Orpheus

No one else will I sing for,
No one else will I love,
No one else will I long for,
No one else here will I love.

These lonely feet trudge through cursed days
without you.
Leaving traces of bitter tears fallen on dusty
roads –
Past our place. Eurydice is gone,
Bitten by death in a heaven-made olive grove –

No one else will I sing for,
No one else will I love.
No one else will I long for.
No one else here – only our love.

I travelled across the Styx to find her,
Bring my Eurydice home.
My lonely voice howls,
Deep in the hollow of Charon's shadow –
I have nowhere else to go.

My courage fails as lyre strings slash my
fingertips,
These grieving songs of us cannot face the sun.

Men, who once adored my tales
now jeer and curse as I tell of our ill-fated love,
Sing of the sorrows that have befallen us.

No one else will I sing for,
No one else will I love.
No one else – will I long for.
No one else here, only my love.

Be careful where you stand, my love,
Be careful in Hades halls –
As you wait for me in the silence.

No one else will I sing for.
No one else will I love.

Daedalus

These old eyes, helpless and blue as the sea,
into which plummeted my most-beloved son.
Featherless, he fell –
I wished it had been me.

I, who built those wings.
It was I who concocted the plan.
Now, my beloved son is dead –
By my own careless hand.

Freedom, was our dream –
But Icarus, oh my beloved son
who flew too far, flew too high –
Now rests in Poseidon's kingdom.

My beloved son –
for all time destined to die.

Elpis

I am the light,
That you cannot see,
When you sit under the moonless dark,
Needing company.

I am the love,
When you feel none at all,
When the days are too tough,
And you feel small.

I am the light,
Walk by me, and take my hand,
Together, let's adventure,
To some distant undiscovered land.

I am hope,
In me place your fears,
I'll help you onwards,
past the tracks of your
tears.